W9-ASV-878

100 QUESTIONS about BUGS

and all the answers too!

Written and Illustrated by
Simon Abbott

PETER PAUPER PRESS, INC.
White Plains, New York

PETER PAUPER PRESS

In 1928, at the age of twenty-two, Peter Beilenson began printing books on a small press in the basement of his parents' home in Larchmont, New York. Peter—and later, his wife, Edna—sought to create fine books that sold at "prices even a pauper could afford."

Today, still family owned and operated, Peter Pauper Press continues to honor our founders' legacy of quality, value, and fun for big kids and small kids alike.

For Ellie and George. Bee happy!

Designed by Heather Zschock

Published by Peter Pauper Press, Inc.
202 Mamaroneck Avenue
White Plains, New York 10601 USA

Published in the United Kingdom and Europe by Peter Pauper Press, Inc.
c/o White Pebble International
Unit 2, Plot 11 Terminus Rd.
Chichester, West Sussex PO19 8TX, UK

Library of Congress Cataloging-in-Publication Data Available

ISBN 978-1-4413-2618-8
Manufactured for Peter Pauper Press, Inc.
Printed in Hong Kong

7 6 5 4 3 2 1

Visit us at www.peterpauper.com

WHAT'S THE BUZZ ABOUT BUGS?

Here's a crash course in nature's creepy crawlies.

Get out your magnifying glass and marvel at the biggest, smallest, deadliest, and smelliest specimens. Try to keep up with the beetles that scuttle at break-neck speed!

You'll spot some incredible insects, and ugly bugs that will give you the creeps.

Scurry along and separate the facts from the fiction.

You'll "bee" amazed!

BRILLIANT BUGS!

Welcome to the world of bugs!

How many bugs are on planet Earth?

The animals we think of as bugs are called **arthropods**, and they make up over three quarters of the planet's creatures. You can find them on land, in the air, and in the water. They're hard to count, but scientists have estimated 10 quintillion (or million trillion) for the insects alone. That's 200 million insects for every human!

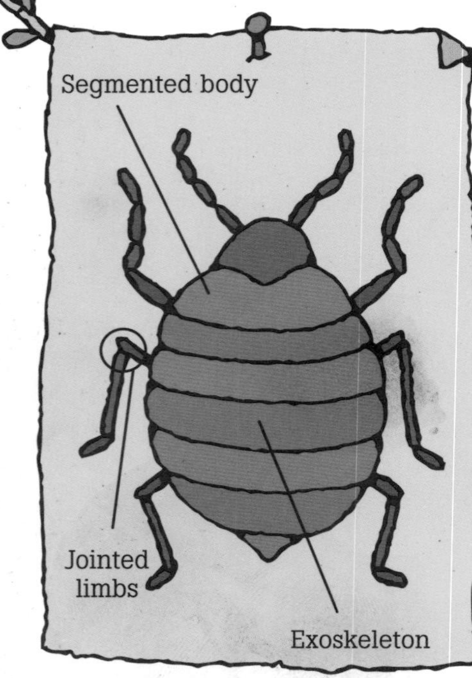

There are millions of types of arthropod, but they have four things in common:

1. A hard outer shell called an **exoskeleton**.
2. They are **invertebrates**, which means they don't have a backbone.
3. A **segmented** body, with separate parts linked together.
4. **Jointed** limbs.

Are there any arthropods we don't think of as bugs?

Yup! If it lives in the water, we often don't call it a bug. Many arthropod swimmers are crustaceans, like crabs, shrimp, and others. Some weird spider relatives, like horseshoe crabs, also live in the water.

What arthropods DO we call bugs?

Most of the animals we think of as bugs belong to three groups: **insects**, **arachnids**, and **myriapods**.

What makes an insect an insect?

Insects include **ants**, **bees**, **ladybugs**, and many more. An insect's body has three sections, six jointed legs, and a pair of antennae on the head. They usually have wings and can fly. Now scoot along!

What are arachnids?

Well, you've heard of **spiders**, which are the most famous bugs in this group. You'll find **scorpions**, **mites**, **harvestmen**, and **ticks** here too! They have eight legs and two main body parts. They don't have antennae or wings.

Arachnid

What makes myriapods different?

This group boasts around 15,000 species and includes **millipedes**, **centipedes**, and others. They are famous for their many pairs of legs, with some species having up to 750. That's a lot of socks!

These bugs have two main body sections, a pair of antennae on their head, and jaw-like mouthparts.

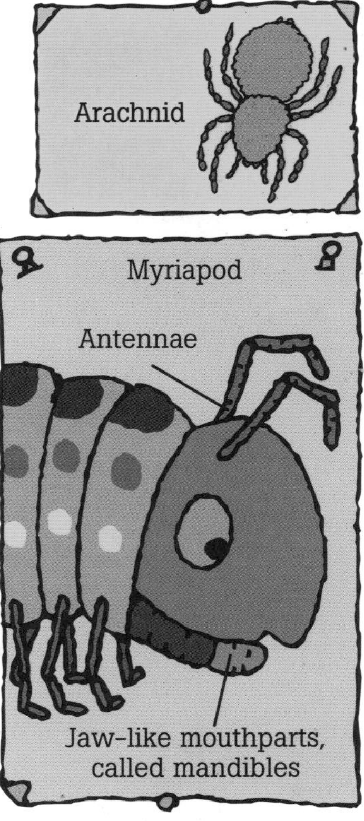

Why did the fly never land on the computer?

He was afraid of the world wide web!

LIFE AS A BUG

Check out the wild ways bugs eat, smell, breathe, and more!

What are an insect's body parts called?

The three sections are the **head**, **thorax**, and **abdomen**.

How are insect eyes different from human eyes?

A human eye has a single lens, but most insects have **compound eyes** made from thousands of tightly-packed mini lenses, giving them an awesome wide view.

What are antennae for?

They double as a bug's nose and, among other things, can smell. A bug waggles and waves them, touching its surroundings. This helps bugs find food, avoid predators, and meet mates!

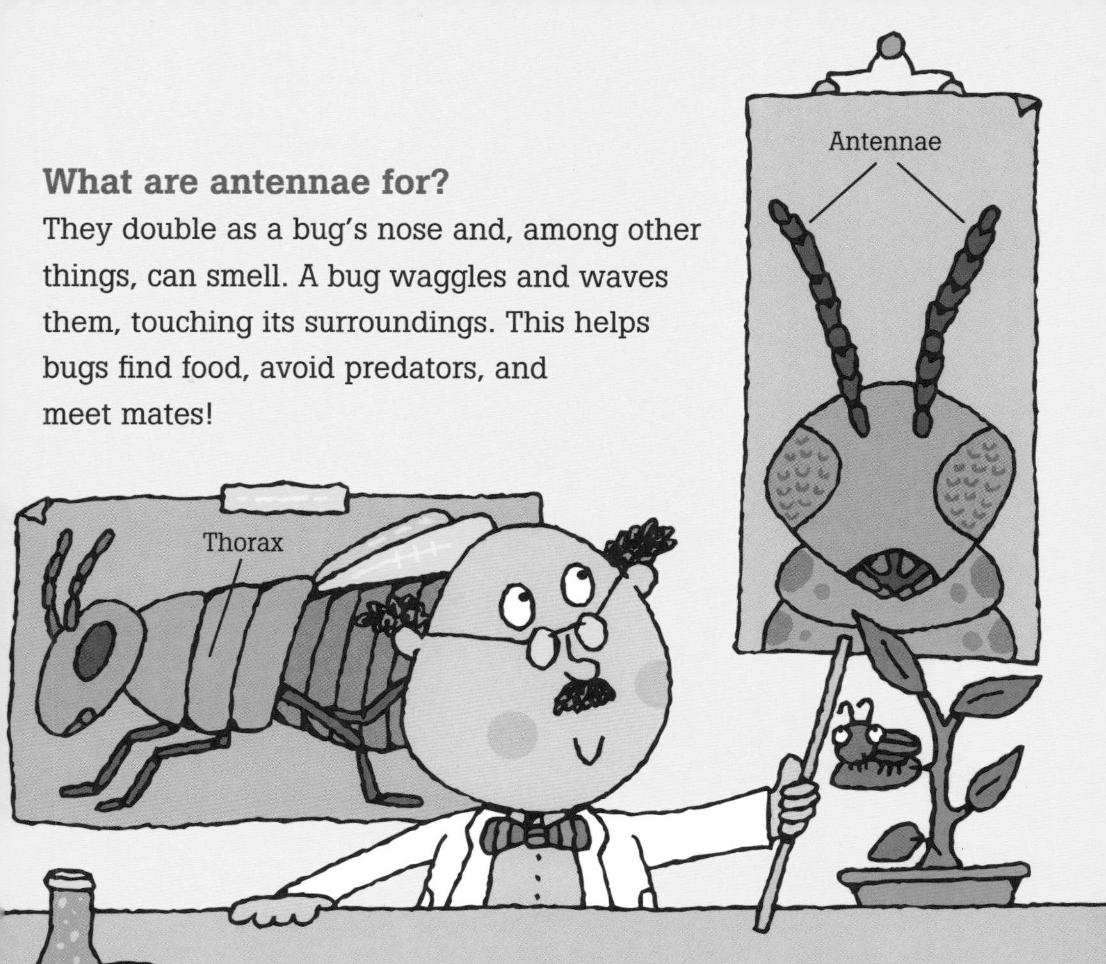

Do bugs have bones inside their bodies?

Nope! Their bodies are supported from the outside by the **exoskeleton**, a hard shell made of strong and flexible stuff called chitin. It provides protection, but allows the bug to scuttle, scurry, and fly freely!

What happens to the exoskeleton when a bug gets bigger?

The exoskeleton does not grow with the bug. Growing bugs break out of their protective casing, then expand to their new size before the new exoskeleton hardens. This process is called **molting**. Bet you wished that happened with t-shirts!

How about arachnids? What's the low-down on these eight-legged legends?

They have two body parts called the **abdomen** and the **cephalothorax**. They have four pairs of legs, and two more limbs called **pedipalps**, which they use to hold and crush their dinner!

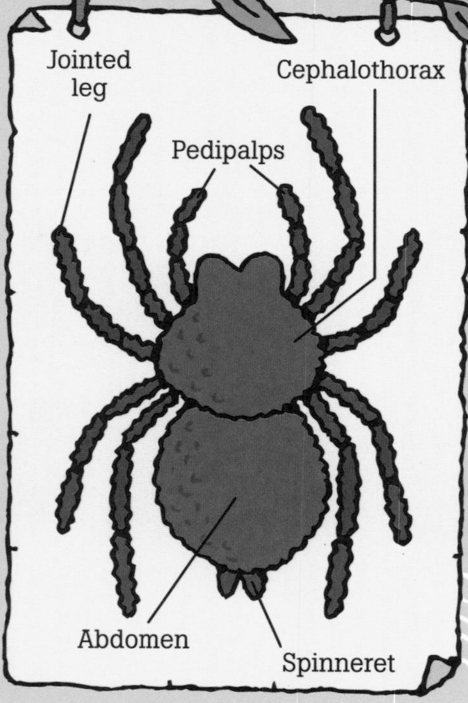

What do spiders make their webs out of?

They spin them with **spider silk**, created in a gland called the **spinneret**! In addition to weaving sticky traps for their prey, spiders may use threads of silk to climb, line their burrows, find their way home, protect their eggs, and mummify the victims they catch.

Do spiders have compound eyes like insects?

No, they have single lens eyes. Most spiders have eight, but some have six, four, two, and even none! Spiders cannot move their eyes to look around. Instead, they use the hair on their legs to feel their way around, and sense vibrations and air movement to "hear" predators or victims nearby.

What about myriapods? Are they like other bugs?

Well, they have an exoskeleton like all arthropods, two main body portions like a spider, and antennae like an insect. What makes them unique is their many legs. Centipedes sport one pair of legs on each segment, and millipedes have two.

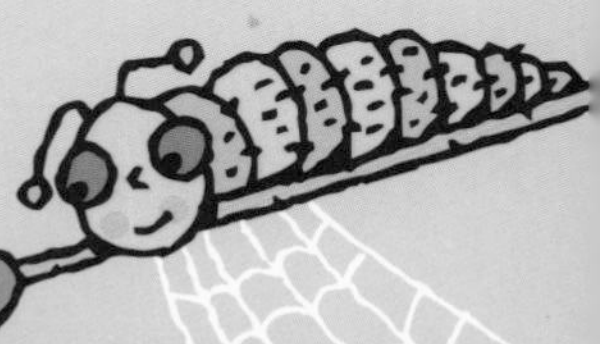

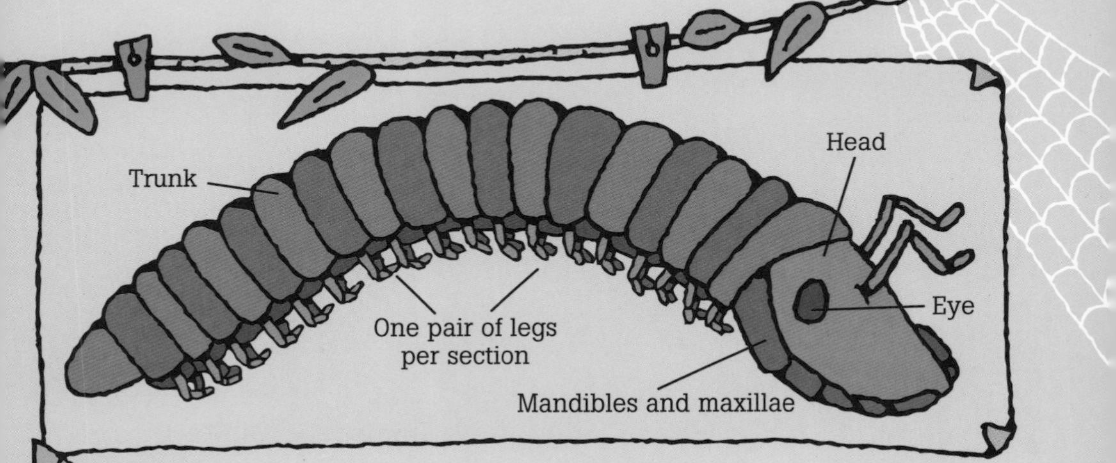

How do myriapods eat?

Like many other bugs, they have parts in their mouth called **mandibles** and **maxillae**, which grab, crush, and chew food. Yum!

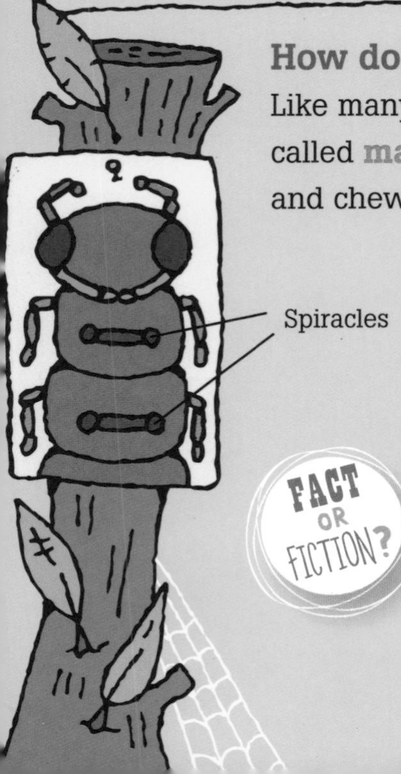

Do myriapods breathe through their mouths?

No. Like most bugs, myriapods take in air through **spiracles**, which are holes in the body wall. Sounds like a hole lot of fun!

PREHISTORIC PALS!

Bugs go way back . . . even before the dinosaurs stomped around our planet! Let's take a peek at these ancient arthropods.

How long have bugs been buzzing their way around?

Scientists have looked at the **fossils**, done the math, and discovered that the first arthropods lived in the sea around **540 million years ago**. These early beasts would have been small swimmers.

What is a fossil?

Fossils are the remains of prehistoric animals or plants, often found in rocks.

Do we REALLY know what ancient bugs looked like?

Yes! Some bugs can be seen in a hard material called **amber**, looking just as they did when they were alive.

What's amber?

Millions of years ago, a sticky, clear liquid called resin dripped from trees in a forest. Some of the drops covered bugs, then over time fossilized into a stone-like substance. The bugs were preserved in this stuff, which we call amber, looking exactly the same as when they died in prehistoric times.

The study of prehistoric bugs is called (deep breath) **paleoentomology**. (Say pal – ee – o – ent – om – ol – o – gee.)

What is the oldest insect ever discovered?

The old-timer's prize goes to the **Rhyniognatha hirsti**. This ancient fellow buzzed around roughly 400 million years ago, in a time called the Devonian Period. Scientists think it was a winged insect that ate plants.

Were there any REALLY HUGE creepy crawlies back then?

Although it lived 300 million years ago, try to imagine this myriapod crawling up your leg. At over eight feet (or 2.5 m) long, **Arthropleura** was the ancient cousin of today's centipedes and millipedes. This friendly fellow only ate plants!

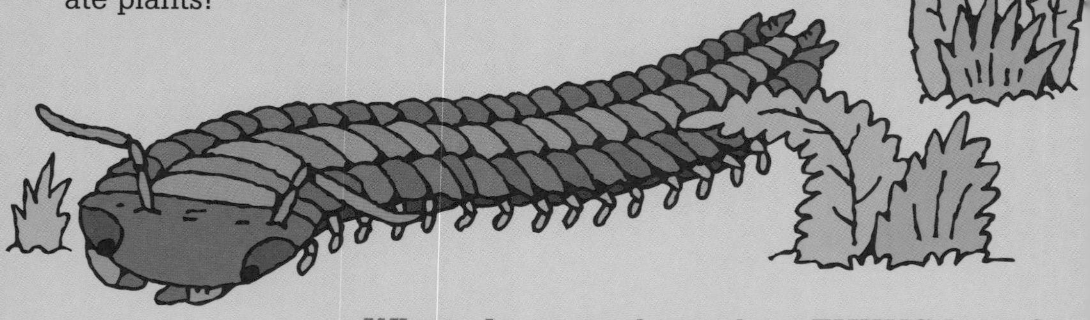

What about ancient giant FLYING bugs?

You'd have a job swatting this bug from bygone days! **Meganeura** was a gigantic dragonfly-like beast from the Carboniferous period (300 million years ago). With a two-foot (61 cm) wingspan and a 17-inch (43 cm) body, scientists think this creature snacked on pretty big prey to keep its energy up!

Did any arachnids get colossal?

One of the biggest arachnids of all time was **Pulmonoscorpious kirktonensis**. (No, I haven't just hit all the keys on the keyboard . . . it means lung scorpion!) This super-sized specimen measured over 27 inches (69 cm) from its head to the tip of its sting. That's longer than two boxes of cereal, but not as tasty!

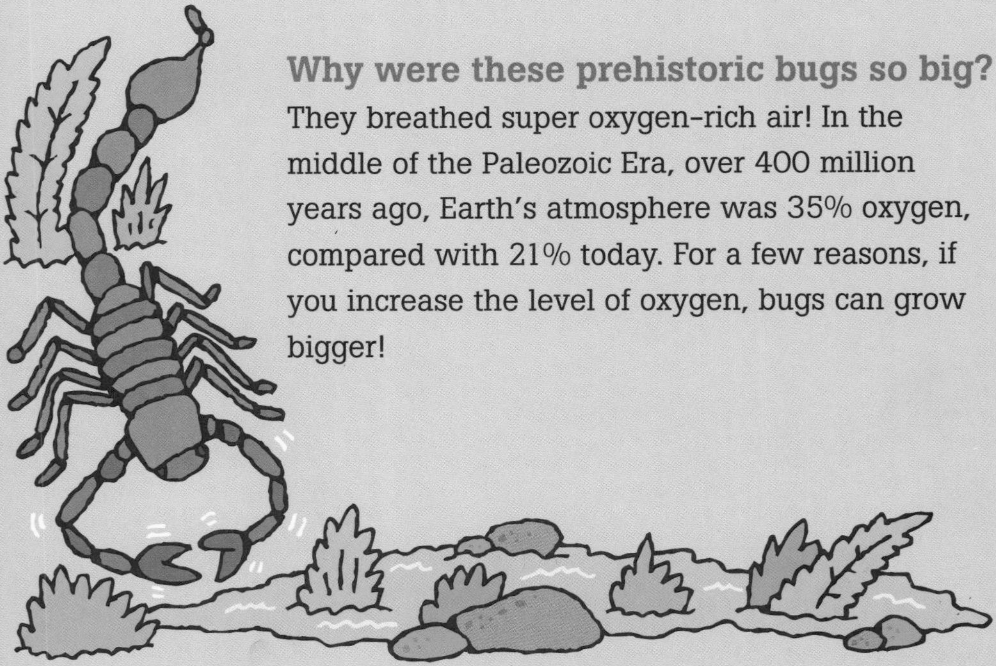

Why were these prehistoric bugs so big?

They breathed super oxygen-rich air! In the middle of the Paleozoic Era, over 400 million years ago, Earth's atmosphere was 35% oxygen, compared with 21% today. For a few reasons, if you increase the level of oxygen, bugs can grow bigger!

Final question . . . are these giant bugs still bothering us today?

No need to check under your bed. Dragonflies of doom and mammoth myriapods are a thing of the past! The first round of really big bugs bit the dust when Earth's oxygen levels dropped.

For most of bug history, insects got bigger when oxygen levels rose. But scientists think that changed when new predators took to the skies. Fast, hungry pterosaurs (flying reptiles) launched into the air, followed by even faster birds. Insects had to get small and zippy to escape!

BIG, SMALL, AND HARDLY THERE AT ALL!

It's time to hand out the prizes to the largest, smallest, heaviest, and longest bugs. Let the contest begin!

What's the world's longest insect?

That prize goes to a stick insect, named **Phryganistria chinensis Zhao**, discovered in China in 2016. This skinny specimen measured an impressive 24.5 inches (62 cm) long. That's longer than two American footballs end-to-end!

How big is the world's largest caterpillar?

The **hickory horned devil** can grow up to 6 inches (15 cm) long. That's roughly as long as a dollar bill! Although their spikes make them look scary, they are harmless. Thank goodness!

How small is the world's tiniest insect?

Get out your magnifying glass! **Fairyflies**, also known as fairy wasps, are on average 0.03 inches (0.08 cm) long, although one has been found that measured just 0.005 inches (0.013 cm)! That's even smaller than the period at the end of this sentence.

FACT OR FICTION?

Are some spiders REALLY as big as dinner plates?

It's true! The **Goliath bird-eating spider** has a record leg span of 11 inches (28 cm). It's often found in South American rainforests, if you want to pop by and say "hello!"

. . . and does the Goliath bird-eating spider spin the world's biggest web?

Well, no. That honor goes to **Darwin's bark spider**. Even though they're small spiders, these creepy crawlies weave webs with threads over 82 feet (25 m) long. That's longer than a bowling lane!

Which butterfly has the largest wings?

Its name is **Queen Alexandra's birdwing**, and it has a wingspan of a foot (30 cm). That's longer than a piece of printer paper!

READY, SET, GO!

Who are the fastest sprinters on six legs, and who can hardly crawl out of bed? Get out your stopwatches and head to the bug racetrack!

If all the bugs in the world ran a race, who would come in third place?

The bronze medal would probably go to the **tiger moth caterpillar**. This sporting star has been recorded traveling at an impressive 3.1 miles per hour (5 kph)!

Which bug would score second place silver?

Let's hear it for the **American cockroach**, who can run a remarkable 3.4 miles per hour (5.5 kph). This superbug is able to fly (but hardly ever bothers) and can live for a whole week without a head! That's some party trick!

Who would win the title of world's fastest bug?

The gold medal goes to the **Australian tiger beetle**. In 1996 two scientists recorded it running at a whopping 5.6 miles per hour (9 kph)!

Can you give me the low-down on this world-class wonder?

Tiger beetles chow down on any unfortunate bug they happen to spot. They are equipped with enormous jaws (called mandibles), which they use to crush and cut their prey. If that isn't bad enough, they spit juices onto their victims while chewing them to hurry along the digestive process, then suck up the gruesome gloop!

Does this speedy superstar wear glasses?

Nope! However, the tiger beetle runs SO fast that it is unable to see once moving! It has to "lock on" to its victims first, or run in short bursts to keep an eye on its prey. "Eye" don't believe it!

READY FOR TAKEOFF!

Fasten your seatbelts . . . we're going for a ride! Introducing the gold medal jumpers and the first-class flyers!

Were insects the first creatures to take flight?

It's true! In order to reach the food that other creatures couldn't get to, and make a quick escape from enemies, insects developed the ability to fly over 360 million years ago.

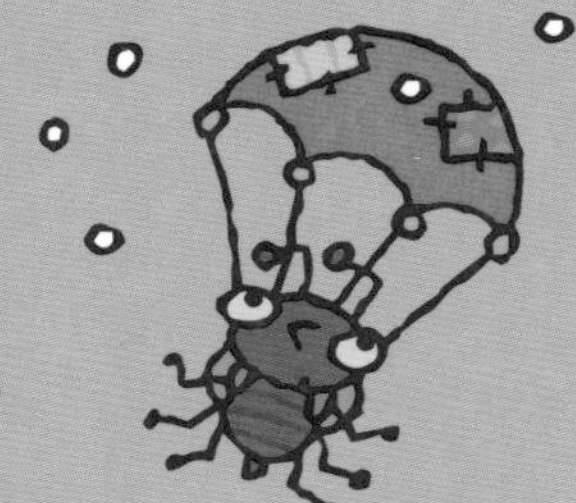

How high can insects fly?

Some insects have a real head for heights! **Bumblebees** can fly as high as Mount Everest at a mind-blowing 18,000 feet (5,500 m)! However, the winner is a tough little **termite** that was caught in an airplane's insect trap at 19,000 feet (5,800 m). That's one way to hitch a ride!

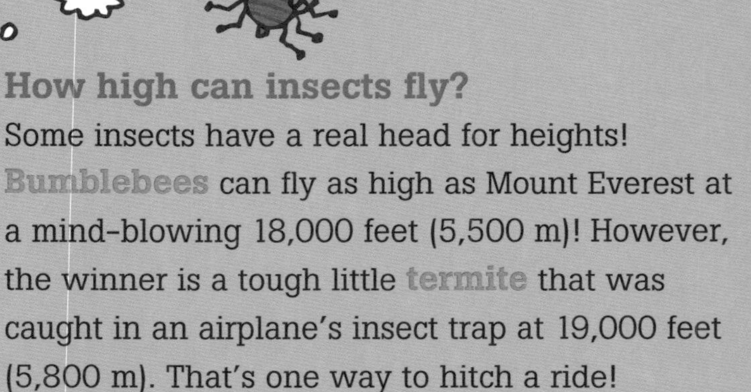

Which speedy bug has recorded the fastest flight?

The **horsefly** has flown at 90.5 miles per hour (145.6 kph). This brave bug even chased, caught, and dropped a pellet from an airgun mid-flight! What a guy!

What bug holds the crown for the world's longest flight?

Snatching the crown from the **monarch butterfly** comes the **"winged wanderer" dragonfly**. This fearsome flyer travels over 11,000 miles (17,700 km), searching for pools to lay its eggs. We don't know exactly what path it takes, as tracking devices are too big for the dragonfly's tiny body. Let's hope they get an in-flight movie!

Which bug is the funniest flyer?

That award goes to the **Hercules beetle**, better known as the "helicopter bug." It looks like a helicopter and it sounds like a helicopter! Unfortunately, this super-sized specimen is rather heavy, so it's not the most able aviator!

How high has an insect jumped?

The highest leap belongs to the **froghopper**, a humble farm pest. This little fellow grows to just ¼ inch (½ cm) long, but has jumped 28 feet (8.5 m). That's like a six-foot (183 cm) man leaping across two American football fields end to end. How high can you get?

How do you start an insect race?

Flea...two...one...GO!

LOUD AND CLEAR!

Did you think all bugs were silent? Think again! Let's meet the rowdy rascals of the arthropod world.

Think noisy insects, think crickets! Why do these ear-popping pests make such a commotion?

Male crickets chirp to attract females, and to warn male competition to stay away. The bottom of their left wing is ribbed, and is called the file. The top part of the right wing is called the scraper. When these two parts rub together, it creates a sound. This process is called "stridulation." (And if you can't sleep at night it's called VERY annoying!)

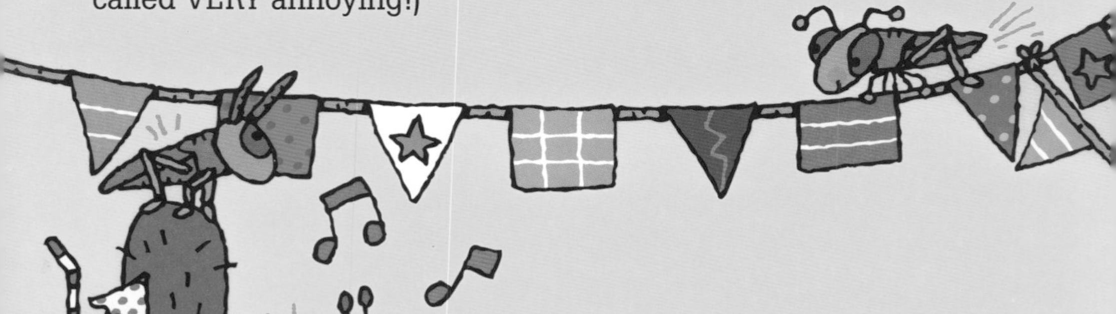

Do some insects hiss?

Yes, it's true! There is a kind of cockroach from Madagascar called the "Gromphadorhinini." (Try to pronounce that!) When two males are fighting for the affections of the female, they hiss like crazy. The roach with the most powerful performance wins the day!

What's the loudest bug around?

The water boatman is only 0.08 inches (.20 cm) long, but pound for pound is the noisiest creature on the planet! This ear-blasting bug can achieve 99.2 decibels in an effort to attract a mate. That's as loud as a garbage truck! Thankfully, the water boatman is muted, as he lives underwater. But his call can still be heard on the riverbank. Shhhhhhh!

Which bug makes the sweetest sound?

That would be the wolf spider, who rubs its pedipalps (remember them?) together to create a "purring" vibration. This is used to court and charm his female companion. Ah, love!

Are any booming bugs as loud as a rock concert?

The clicks and chirps from a male cicada are so loud they can be heard by the females a mile away! These grasshopper-like insects produce sounds of over 120 decibels by vibrating membranes called tymbals. Time to turn over the page for some peace and quiet!

HERE COMES TROUBLE!

Here's the buzz on the world's deadliest bugs. Don't say we didn't warn you!

What has antlers and sucks blood?

WARNING!

Should I be worried?

How many bugs are dangerous?

Chill! They're not all out to get you! Only a tiny percentage of bugs are harmful to humans.

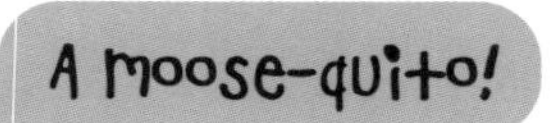

What's the difference between poison and venom?

If a creature bites or stings you with a toxin, that's venom. Venomous bugs include **black widow spiders** and **hornets**. If a bug delivers its toxins when you eat or touch it, that's poison. **Stinging caterpillars** and **blister beetles** are members of the poisonous bug brigade.

Which is the deadliest species on Earth?

The most lethal killer doesn't use poison OR venom. **Mosquitos** cause half a million deaths each year by spreading malaria parasites. There are no vaccines for malaria, but anti-malarial tablets and mosquito nets can protect people. Phew!

BUZZ off!

Killer bees sound fairly ferocious! How can I avoid them?

Start running! Groups of **killer bees**, or Africanized honeybees, can chase their victims for more than a mile, stinging the victim's face and eyes. They are smaller than run-of-the-mill honeybees, and their venom is less powerful, but they attack in huge numbers if their hive is disturbed.

Does the bullet ant look like a bullet?

No! It's called the **bullet ant** because its sting is as painful as being shot, and the pain lasts a full day.

So, it's one I should steer clear of?

Definitely, unless you're a member of the Satere-Mawe tribe in Brazil. Their initiation ceremony for young warriors involves wearing a glove full of bullet ants for a torturous 10 minutes. Arghhhh!

Which spider should I keep an eye out for?

One scary specimen is the **six-eyed sand spider**. (Try saying that 10 times in a hurry!) Its venom is extremely dangerous, and can destroy tissue and organs. The BAD news is . . . there is no antidote. The GOOD news is . . . the six-eyed sand spider is famously shy. What a relief!

GREEDY GRUBS AND BLOODTHIRSTY BUGS!

These bugs are hardhearted hunters!

What's a predatory bug?

A predatory bug eats other bugs, sometimes as well as fish, lizards, and even mammals. They are skillful hunters!

Who are the top predators?

First up, let's hear it for the **praying mantis**. This bug has two front legs lined with hooks and spines to catch hold of its victim. It lies low, then grabs its prey with a lightning-fast leap. Gotcha!

What other methods do these cunning creatures employ?

The **assassin bug** hides itself with a disguise of dust, bark, or dead insects. Once its victim is within reach, it uses its needle-like mouthparts to inject a lethal saliva. Game over!

Does this predator have any other tricks?

The ant-eating kind of assassin bug is a smart operator. It oozes a sweet liquid, attracting sugar-loving ants. This liquid is loaded with a strong tranquilizer, which paralyzes the helpless ants. The assassin bug can suck out its victims' innards without a care in the world.

Are cute ladybugs really creepy-crawly killing machines?

It's true! **Ladybugs** gorge on mites and aphids, helping to fight the battle against garden pests.

Who are the tough arachnid predators?

Jumping spiders don't hang out in webs waiting for dinner to arrive. They lunge at their prey, spinning out a silk safety rope in case they miss the target. Some jumping spiders can leap 40 times their own length. That's the same as a human hopping five school buses!

Yikes!

How do you spot a modern spider?

He doesn't have a web—he has a website!

WE'RE MOVING IN!

Don't put out the welcome mat for these bloodthirsty parasites! They have a nasty habit of bedding down where they're not wanted.

What's the deal with parasites?

Parasites are bugs that live on or in another creature, called the "host." They depend on their host for food, and although they can harm the host, they rarely kill it.

Are there any parasites that DO kill?

Afraid so! These irritating bugs are called **parasitoids.**

Can you give me an example?

Female **Glyptapanteles wasps** inject their eggs into living caterpillars. The eggs develop into larvae, which grow by eating the caterpillar's body. As a group, the larvae chomp through the host's skin, emerge, then move on to the next stage of their lives. Nice knowing you!

Do humans get troubled by blood-sucking bugs?

Yes! The **paralysis tick** is really unpleasant. It hangs around on leaves with its legs stretched out, just waiting to grab an unsuspecting victim. It latches onto the host, ballooning up as it sucks up blood. Paralysis ticks can pass on diseases, and can inject a paralyzing toxin. Not nice!

Do any parasitic bugs live inside people?

Well, stay clear of the **human botfly**! This bug captures mosquitoes and lays its eggs on their bodies. Soon, the mosquito finds a human to feed from. The eggs fall onto the human victim and hatch. The botfly maggot will tunnel into the human's skin and set up home for 6 weeks.

Tell me more! What happens then?

If left alone, the maggot will re-emerge through the hole, drop to the ground, and continue growing into an adult botfly. Then the whole cycle begins again!

What's green and jumps a mile per minute?

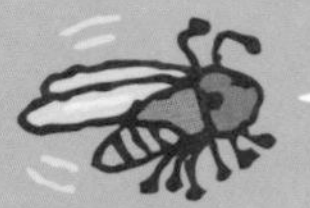

A grasshopper with the hiccups!

BUSY BEES AND SPINNING SILKWORMS!

Many bugs have important jobs.
Take a look at the helpful heroes of the bug world.

Which bugs are helpful and handy?

Let's start with the honeybee! Honeybees are part of an incredibly important group of animals called pollinators. They transfer pollen between the male and female parts of plants, allowing the plants to grow, make seeds, and produce fruit. Honeybees gather nectar and pollen from flowers, then store it in honey and beeswax to feed their colony. Human beekeepers take care of honeybee colonies, and harvest the extra honey they make!

How long have humans been keeping bees?

Over 9,000 years! Archaeologists discovered that farmers in Turkey were using beeswax in 7,000 BC. Un-bee-lievable!

Is honey-making an easy process?

Hardly! To produce just ONE pound of honey, bees visit 2 million flowers, and 55,000 miles (88,500 km) are flown by the whole hive. An average worker bee makes just 1/12 teaspoon of honey in her lifetime! They should get up earlier!

TAX OFFICE

Is that why honey is expensive?

It always has been. The ancient Romans sometimes paid their taxes in honey, not gold!

Are any bugs welcome garden visitors, instead of plant-eating pests?

Of course! The black and yellow garden spider is a great friend to gardeners. It feasts on a diet of garden pests and helps control flies, moths, beetles . . . even grasshoppers! The big dipper firefly's larvae help out by dining on destructive slugs and snails.

What other bugs are helpful in a garden?

The green lacewing is a hero of the vegetable patch. This greedy predator will devour over 200 insects a week. Gulp!

Fancy!

Is silk REALLY spun by silkworms?

Yes! So-called silkworms are caterpillars, and create their cocoons from a single silk thread that can measure over 3,000 feet (915 m) long. That could reach a third of the way over the Golden Gate Bridge!

How do bees brush their hair?

With a honeycomb!

SHAPE SHIFTERS!

Becoming an adult is rarely easy. For some bugs the changes are impressive!

Baby humans look like tiny versions of grown-up humans. Do baby insects look like grown-up insects?

Not usually! Most insects have four stages in their life cycle:

1. **The egg**: A tiny oval or cylinder.
2. **The larva**: A baby insect, often looking a little like a worm, which eats and grows.
3. **The pupa**: A stage for big changes, when the adult insect's body is built.
4. **The adult**: The adult comes out of the pupa, can move around, and can lay eggs.

Does this process have a name?

Yes! It's called **metamorphosis**, from the Greek word "metamorphoun," meaning to transform or change shape.

Do all insects go through these four stages?

No. Insects such as dragonflies, grasshoppers, and cock-roaches miss out on the pupa stage of the cycle, and undergo **incomplete metamorphosis**. That speeds things up a bit! Some primitive insects, like silverfish, don't metamorphose at all, and simply grow larger over time. These are called **ametabolous**.

How long does metamorphosis take?

Let's look at the butterfly as an example. The egg hatches after four or five days and a tiny larva, or caterpillar, appears. The larva starts to eat, and as it grows, sheds its skin up to six times. It takes about three weeks for the larva to be fully grown, and to transform into a pupa, or chrysalis.

What happens next?

Inside the chrysalis, the caterpillar takes itself apart and rebuilds itself into the adult body of the butterfly. This stage can take 10 to 15 days. Finally, the adult butterfly emerges from the pupa, and is free to fly!

Do spiders lay eggs too?

They do! The female lays thousands of eggs in silken sacs, which are often attached to webs, or hidden in nests for protection. Some spiders carry the sacs, or stick them to their spinnerets and drag them along. Sounds exhausting!

Do spiders hatch as larvae?

No! Young **spiderlings** hatch looking like mini adults, but don't have fully adult bodies. Some spiderlings are left alone, and have been known to eat each other! Other babies climb onto the mother's back where she cares for them. They hop off when they're ready!

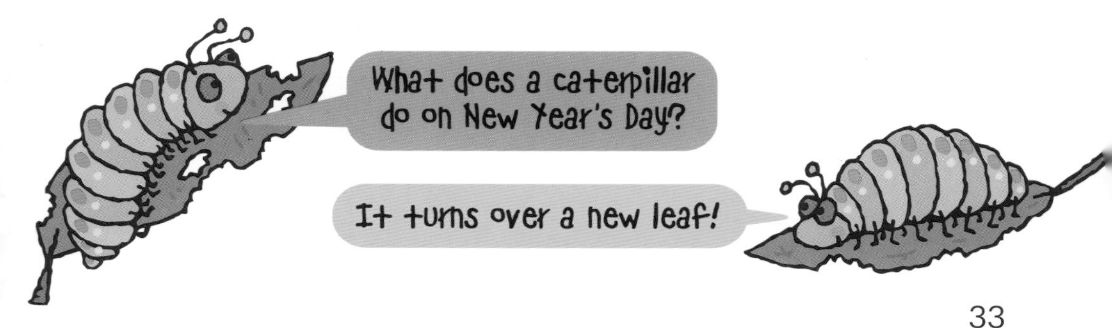

IT TAKES A VILLAGE!

Let's look inside the world of insect colonies, where only the most sociable creatures feel at home!

Which insects live in colonies?

Ants, for starters! Ants are social insects who create colonies in plants, wood, below ground, and elsewhere. These super-efficient communities are most often ruled by a single queen, and taken care of by worker ants and soldier ants. Attention!

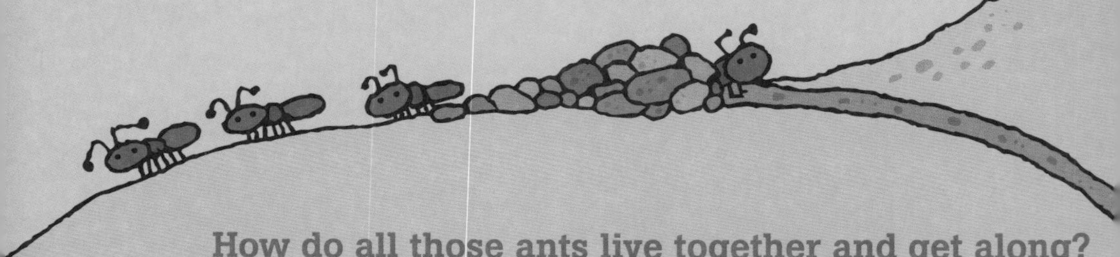

How do all those ants live together and get along?

They share the work of keeping the colony alive! Each ant has a job, starting with the queen. A queen's job is to lay eggs, and the male ants' job is to mate with her (then die very soon afterwards). Soldier and worker ants protect the queen, defend the colony, and find food. Other ant jobs include looking after the young, gathering the food they find, and building the colony's home.

How does a colony get started?

When she is ready, a new queen ant will leave her original colony, find a fresh location that is warm and safe, dig a small chamber, and lay her eggs. When hatched, the new ants start digging! They remove the dirt piece by piece, carrying it out of the tunnels in their mandibles. This dirt creates anthills!

Can ants build anything else?

Yes—they're smart engineers! If threatened by floods, ants can escape by using their bodies to build rafts and bridges. They even whip up temporary shelters while new colonies are under construction. I c–ant believe it!

Which other insects live in colonies?

LOTS, including **honeybees**! They live in nests made of stacked layers of wax cells. Wild honeybees make their nests in safe, warm places such as rock crevices or hollow trees. 20,000 to 80,000 bees might inhabit a nest!

Do honeybees have a queen?

Yes! She lays thousands of eggs, but the drone bees, who she mates with, will exterminate the queen if she fails to lay enough.

Are some colonies a pain in the neck?

For sure! Some **termites** create their colonies in dry wood (like the stuff houses are made of). On the plus side, it would take one termite over 3,000 years to gnaw through an average home. On the other hand, colonies can contain up to 15,000,000 termites. You win some, you lose some!

FRUIT FLY FLAN AND SPIDER SOUP!

Do folks REALLY eat bugs?

Yes! It's called "entomophagy." Bugs regularly appear on the menus of 2 billion people around the world. Would you gobble up a grass-hopper or crunch a cricket?

Is this a recent trend?

Not at all! Ancient Algerians dined on dried locusts, and Aboriginal Australians have enjoyed honey pot ants and almond-tasting witchety grubs for a long time. Aristotle, the ancient Greek philosopher and scientist, wrote about harvesting delicious cicadas.

Is eating bugs a great idea?

Here are the positives . . .

1. It could help solve world hunger. After all, there are 300 pounds of insects for every pound of human.
2. They provide most necessary nutrients, including protein, calcium, zinc, and iron.
3. Bugs are cheap to produce. Crickets, for instance, need 12 times less feed than cows to produce the same amount of protein.
4. They're all around us! With over 1,000 species edible to humans, there's something for everyone!
5. They've been tried and tested in lots of locations around the world.

Do some countries really dish out these delicacies already?

Yes! Take a look at the menu!

Mexico – chocolate covered locusts

Brazil – fried queen ants

Ghana – roasted termite bread

Thailand – fried grasshoppers

China – roasted bee larvae

The Netherlands – chocolate infused with ground mealworms

Bali – chargrilled dragonfly

Japan – fried silk moth pupae

I'm hungry! Can I grab a bug brunch where I live?

Sure! You might find a restaurant near you with exciting insect entrées. Alternately, you can order online and cook up a storm at home. Recipes include **rootworm beetle dip** and **grasshopper kebabs**. Enjoy!

BIZARRE BEETLES AND FREAKY FLIES!

The bug brigade is full of curious creatures, but some are stranger than others. Let's unearth the world's weirdest!

What baby bugs get a freaky-looking start in life?

The **puss moth caterpillar** is a loathsome-looking larva. This bug's best features are its big black eye spots, and a gaping "mouth," out of which bulges the caterpillar's actual head! If its features don't put you off, the misty spray of formic acid from the two "horns" on its back might do the job!

Puss Moth Caterpillar

Pale Tussock Moth

Are there any fuzzy baby bugs?

The **pale tussock moth caterpillar** is a hairy weirdo! From a distance, this larva looks like a sponge, but don't be fooled! It has a bizarre blend of furry legs, tufts of yellow bristles, dark spine markings, and a double row of mandibles. This weird and wonderful European wriggler is a one-off!

Brazilian Treehopper

How about strange grown-up bugs?

Well, without being rude, the **Brazilian treehopper** might get a shock when it looks in the mirror. With six spindly legs, wings like a locust, and twig-like headgear covered in lumps and bumps, the treehopper is one kooky creepy crawly!

Do some oddballs look like a mash-up of different bugs?

Check out the **scorpionfly**! This funky insect looks like the result of a mad science experiment. It's a fly with what seems like a scorpion's tail on its hind end. We should respect our elders, though. This curious creature has been around since the Permian period, almost 300 million years ago. Sorry, old-timer!

Scorpionfly

What do you get when you cross a centipede with a parrot?

A walkie-talkie!

What about bugs that don't look like bugs at all? What's their story?

Some bugs are masters of disguise, blending perfectly into their surroundings to hide from predators or surprise prey. Let's hear it for the **bird dung crab spider**! This creature's texture and body markings let it imitate bird poop. How chic!

That's a gross but genius strategy. Are there any other poop impersonators?

Celaenia excavata may have a fancy name, but it's commonly called the **bird dropping spider**. This Australian native avoids being attacked by sitting motionless on a leaf all day, pretending to be an unappealing poop. They should try branching out!

Do any weirdo bugs get really big?

Take a peep at the legendary **Hercules beetle**, which can grow more than 6 inches (15 cm) long and sports huge horn-like pincers. These allow the beetle to carry loads up to 850 times its own body weight. That's like a man carrying 30 rhinoceros!

That's pretty big, but what wacky bug is even bigger?

It's giant! It's prickly! It's the **giant prickly stick insect**! This 8-inch (20 cm) bug is covered with giant thorn-like spikes, and is skilled in the art of camouflage. If in danger, the insect will impersonate a scorpion by curling its tail over its head. They also deter pesky predators by spraying a defensive odor that smells like peanut butter. Mmmmm!

KICKING UP A STINK!

Hold your nose and discover the stinkiest bugs. It's time to spot the smelly squad!

Why do some bugs smell?

That's not very polite! Some bugs give off an odor to attract a mate, and others just spend their lives around dung. For some bugs, it's a defense system. No one wants to eat something that stinks! Certain millipedes use unique scents to say "back off," like a cherry-cola-smelling cyanide. Nice!

What bugs spend their lives around dung?

Dung beetles find poop, roll balls of poop, eat poop, and line their nests with poop! They've been doing it for 30 million years too! Fossilized dung balls the size of tennis balls have been discovered in South America.

Wait a second! Do they actually eat poop?

Yes! Dung beetles squeeze poop in their mouths, then slurp the juice. A nutrient-packed smoothie!

How do they move all that poop around?

They're among the world's strongest insects! The beetles roll dung into balls that weigh over 50 times their own body weight. The record goes to an *Onthophagus taurus* dung beetle that shifted a load 1,141 times its weight. That's like a 150-pound (68 kg) human hauling your house!

Do stink bugs stink?

When these insects are under attack, they release a gross odor that smells like sweaty feet or spicy vegetables. Breathe in!

Are any smelly bugs dangerous?

Don't get close to a **bombardier beetle**! If they're disturbed, these ground beetles eject a foul-smelling boiling-hot chemical spray. The spray explodes with a powerful popping sound.

What other smelly bugs shouldn't I mess with?

When predators try and take a bite, the **shore earwig** squirts a stinky substance into the attacker's mouth. This goo smells like rotting flesh, and makes the predator think twice about its dinner plans!

Do bugs themselves have a sense of smell?

Yes! Bugs' sense of smell can be used to find a mate, target prey, avoid attack, and even find somewhere to live. Most insects and myriapods smell through their antennae. They even wipe away dust, wax, and other gunk from their antennae so they can smell stuff better. Spiders smell through organs on their legs.

GLOWING IN THE DARK

These bugs make the night a little brighter!

Is there a word for light-up animals?

Living things that make light are called **bioluminescent**. Most bioluminescent bugs create light with a chemical reaction in their bodies.

Why do bugs light up?

A bug might glow to attract a mate, warn predators to **STAY AWAY!**, and lure prey close enough to chomp.

Where would I see a bioluminescent bug?

Your best chance is at night, when many light-up bugs are active and you'll spot the glow clearly! Some glowing animals also hang out in dark places like caves.

Is a glow-worm bioluminescent?

Yup! But they're not worms. People call a bunch of insects "glow-worms," from gnat larvae to beetles. One type of glow-worm, the luminous **click beetle** larva, burrows into the ground with just its glowing head visible and its jaws open wide. Dazzled by the light, its prey scurries into the sly larva's mouth, and the jaws slam shut!

If a glow-worm isn't really a worm, is a firefly really a fly?

Another case of mistaken identity! These shiny critters, also called "lightning bugs," are beetles as well.

What do they do with their light?

Mostly, they use it to meet a mate! The males flash their light in a specific pattern as a signal. If a female firefly is interested she will flash the code back, helping her mate find her.

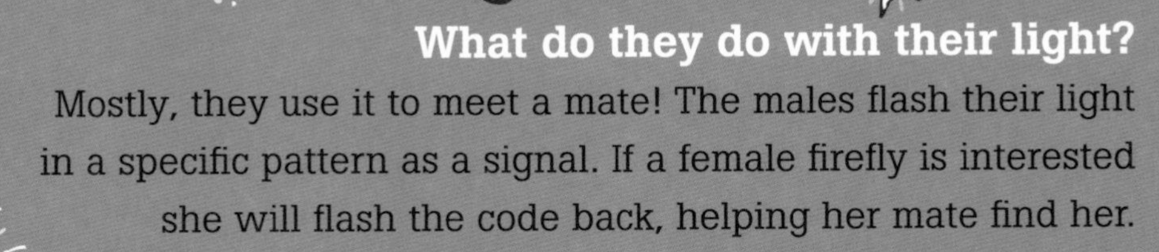

FACT OR FICTION?

Does a firefly shine as bright as a lightbulb?

False! It would take 70,000 fireflies to produce as much light as one lightbulb, but they're trying their best!

What's the brightest bug?

The shining star award goes to the cucujo or **Jamaican click beetle**. This bright beetle has two "headlights" that give off a constant neon green glow. Cool!

How do fireflies start a race?

Ready, Set, Glow!

TICKLY TRUTHS AND MOTH-EATEN MYTHS!

It's time to separate fact from fiction about our bug friends.

Is it true that we swallow spiders in our sleep?

There's a myth that 25% of the protein in our diet is from digesting spiders that crawl into our mouths as we're snoozing. This NEVER happens! It's doubtful you'd ever swallow a spider while you're dozing in your entire life!

Do all spiders spin webs?

No, but they all produce silk. Some spiders live in burrows, and line these habitats with silk, rather than hang around on a web.

Do insects feel pain?

Probably not. They have a pretty basic nervous system, and don't do a lot of the things other animals do when in pain. It might vary from species to species, though.

Do all bees die after they sting you?

No, only if it's a **honeybee**. After it stings you it leaves behind not only the stinger, but parts of its abdomen, digestive tract, and some muscles and nerves. It can't survive after that!

Does a female black widow spider always eat the male?

This myth is only partly true. There are many species of widow spider, and most of the time the gals and the guys get along fine. There are exceptions, and, with certain types of female black widow spiders weighing up to 160 times as much as males, sometimes one does chow down!

Could a cockroach survive a nuclear war?

It's unlikely, but let's hope we never find out! They do have a higher resistance to radiation than humans, but they're no more immune to nuclear fallout than other insects.

What if a cockroach loses its head? Can it survive an accidental decapitation?

Yes! They can scuttle around headless for a couple of weeks. Cockroaches breathe through spiracles all around their body, and don't bleed like humans do. This bug means business!

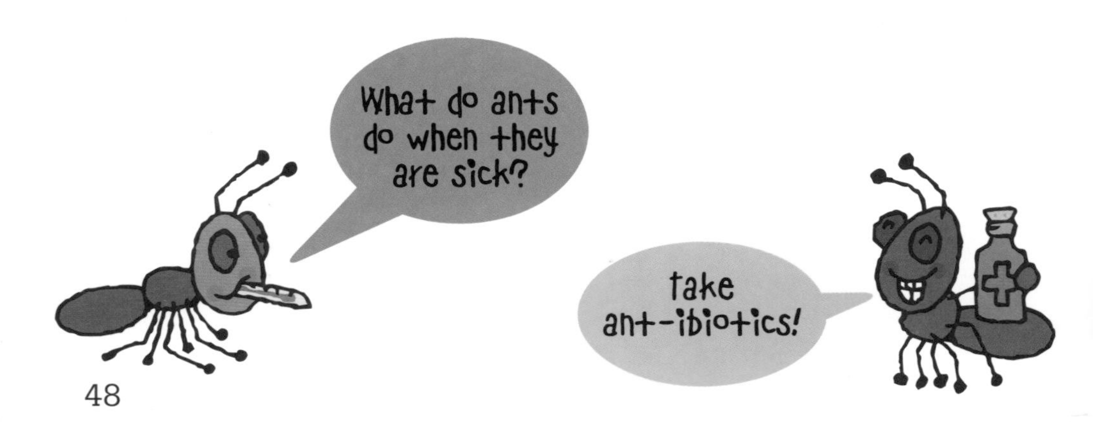

CHECK OUT ALL OF THE FANTASTIC FACTS IN THIS SENSATIONAL SERIES!

100 Questions about Bugs

100 Questions about Colonial America

100 Questions about Outer Space

100 Questions about Pirates